Michelle Koch

WORLD WATER WATCH

Greenwillow Books, New York

Watercolor paints were used for the full-color art.
The text type is ITC Zapf International Medium.

Library of Congress Cataloging-in-Publication Data
Koch, Michelle.
World water watch / by Michelle Koch.
p.   cm.
Summary: Briefly describes some of the dangers caused
mainly by humans for such animals as otters,
sea turtles, seals, penguins, polar bears, and whales.
ISBN 0-688-11464-4 (trade).
ISBN 0-688-11465-2 (lib. bdg.)
1. Wildlife conservation—Juvenile literature.
2. Man—Influence on nature—Juvenile literature.
[1. Rare animals.   2. Wildlife conservation.
3. Man—Influence on nature.]
I. Title.   QL83.K63   1993
639.9—dc20   91-48371   CIP   AC

For my grandparents —
Helen and Andrew,
Suzanne and John

Watch over the world,

Watch over the water.

Some creatures are dying today.

Care for the earth,
Care for the sea.
So all of our friends can stay.

Sea otters
drift among
the kelp
in the
frigid sea
bordering
my home,
Alaska.

Otters constantly clean their thick fur to keep it airy and light. The air trapped in their coats keeps them warm and prevents them from sinking.

To rest or sleep, otters wrap themselves in kelp. The kelp helps them stay afloat, and they bob along the surface of the water like buoys.

When otters swim through an oil spill, their fur becomes matted and heavy. Some drown, and others become sick from swallowing oil.

Otters cannot survive unless we keep our oceans clean.

Green
sea turtles
paddle
through the
warm ocean
waters near
my country,
Mexico.

Sea turtles have had a hard time surviving. We enjoyed eating their meat. We used their shells as decorations. If turtles managed to reach the beaches and lay their eggs, the eggs were often crushed or stolen by both human and animal predators.

In May 1990 the government of Mexico signed an agreement that ended the killing of all sea turtles in its waters. Special areas were also set aside for turtles to nest. Now more newly hatched turtles live to make the journey from the beaches back to the open sea.

Our green sea turtles once again swim safely in the ocean.

Penguins
waddle
across
the ice
in the land
of frozen
beauty,
Antarctica.

There are penguins that live in warmer temperatures, but most penguins endure the frigid conditions of Antarctica.

Many scientists believe that air pollution and the cutting down of rain forests is warming the earth. They fear that the ice that has covered the north and south poles for millions of years is beginning to melt.

If our colder climates disappear, will the Antarctic
penguins be able to adapt to a warmer environment?

Fur seals
gather
along the
lava rocks
on the
islands
edging
my country,
Chile.

Seals are hunted for their fur and their flesh.
Their beautiful skins are used for coats, purses,
and gloves. Their meat is ground up for pet food.

The Juan Fernandez seal that inhabits the offshore islands
belonging to Chile is now protected by the Chilean government.
But many other fur seals are not so fortunate and are still
being killed in places all over the world.

When every country joins in protecting them,
fur seals will be free to play safely on all beaches.

Polar bears
wander
through
falling snow
searching
for food
in the
northern
regions of
my home,
Norway.

Polar bears roam across the ice and are able to survive
the fiercest blizzards because of their coats of thick fur.

Although the hunting of polar bears is illegal in Norway,
the bears are still in danger because they eat fish
that have been poisoned by pesticides and chemicals.

The continuing struggle of the polar bear to survive is a good example of how the actions of people affect the world's wildlife.

Humpback
whales
blow
in the seas
as they
circle the
island
where
I live,
Maui.

Each winter humpback whales migrate to the warm waters
of the Hawaiian islands to join their mates and have their young.

And year after year more and more tourists, fishermen,
and sailors come to view the whales. Their boats create a
traffic jam for the whales, who must keep dodging them.

Will the whales be forced to leave the
waters of Hawaii and find another home?

Watch over the world,
Watch over the water.
Some creatures are dying today.

Care for the earth,
Care for the sea.
So all of our friends can stay.

WHERE THEY LIVE

Sea otters dive in the waters near Alaska and Russia's Kuril Islands, and along the coasts of Washington, Oregon, and California.

The **Juan Fernandez fur seal** has been found only on a few small islands off the central coast of Chile.

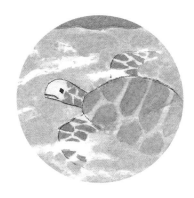

Green sea turtles swim all over the globe in tropical and temperate seas, returning to breed on beaches in Florida, Nicaragua, Mexico, and Costa Rica.

Polar bears roam the frozen ice fields and lands belonging to five nations: Canada, Denmark, Norway, Russia, and the United States.

Eighteen species of **penguins** exist, all surviving in the southern hemisphere. Some live in Antarctica; others are found in southern Australia, New Zealand, and the Galapagos Islands.

Humpback whales can be sighted in all of the world's oceans as they migrate from temperate and subpolar waters in the summer to the tropics in winter.